How Life Science Works

HOW DO BEAVERS MAKE DAMS?

DOROTHY JENNINGS

PowerKiDS press.
New York

Published in 2018 by The Rosen Publishing Group, Inc.
29 East 21st Street, New York, NY 10010

First Edition

Editor: Theresa Morlock
Book Design: Tanya Dellaccio

Photo Credits: Cover, back cover, all pages except p. 2 Robert McGouey/Getty Images; p. 5 (beaver) Perry McKenna Photography/Getty Images; p. 5 (beaver dam) lussiya/Shutterstock.com; p. 7 Jody Ann/Shutterstock.com; p. 9 (beaver) BMJ/Shutterstock.com; p. 9 (Castoroides) https://commons.wikimedia.org/wiki/File:Giant_Pleistocene_Beaver,_Castoroides_ohioensis.jpg; p. 10 Procy/Shutterstock.com; p. 11 Chase Dekker Wild-Life Images/Getty Images; p. 13 (top) Ammit Jack/Shutterstock.com; p. 13 (bottom) SERGEI BRIK/Shutterstock.com; p. 14 Gail Johnson/Shutterstock.com; p. 15 Adwo/Shutterstock.com; p. 17 (beaver hut) Alikosina/Shutterstock.com; p. 17 (beaver family) UbjsP/Shutterstock.com; pp. 18, 19 Dorling Kindersley/Getty Images; p. 19 (beavers) Alan Jeffery/Shutterstock.com; p. 21 (beaver dam) Johannes Dag Mayer/Shutterstock.com; p. 21 (beaver) Vladimir Löwen/EyeEm/Getty Images; p. 22 Zadiraka Evgenii/Shutterstock.com.

Cataloging-in-Publication Data

Names: Jennings, Dorothy.
Title: How do beavers make dams? / Dorothy Jennings.
Description: New York : PowerKids Press, 2017. | Series: How life science works | Includes index.
Identifiers: ISBN 9781508156499 (pbk.) | ISBN 9781508156444 (library bound) | ISBN 9781508156321 (6 pack)
Subjects: LCSH: Beavers—Juvenile literature. | Beavers—Habitations—Juvenile literature.
Classification: LCC QL737.R632 J46 2017 | DDC 599.37—dc23

Manufactured in the United States of America

CPSIA Compliance Information: Batch #BS17PK For Further Information contact Rosen Publishing, New York, New York at 1-800-237-9932

CONTENTS

BUSY AS A BEAVER

Beavers are always working. What exactly are those busy beavers up to? They're chopping down trees, collecting rocks, and gathering mud–they're building a dam!

Beavers are very intelligent creatures. Of all animals, only humans have a better ability to change their environment. Beavers use their skills to **transform** entire landscapes and create ponds where they didn't exist before. They also construct lodges to live in with their families. How do they accomplish these feats of **engineering**? Why do beavers build dams? How exactly do they do it?

Beavers continue their work even under thin layers of ice.

BEAVERS IN HISTORY

Beavers were traditionally treated with respect and admiration by Native Americans. The Huron and Ojibwe people valued beavers for their hard work and cleverness. They hunted beavers for their meat and skins, but only when they needed to.

When Europeans arrived in North America, beavers became the center of the fur trade. People hunted beavers for their pelts, or fur and skin, to sell to fur traders. People liked to make clothes and hats from beaver pelts because they were warm and lasted a long time. By the mid-1800s, North American beavers had almost died out.

During the 1820s, beaver furs went out of fashion as silk became fashionable instead. If that hadn't happened, it's possible that beavers would've died out completely!

BEAVER BASICS

Beavers are rodents, which are mammals with front teeth that never stop growing. They're actually the largest rodents in North America! They can grow up to 31 inches (78.8 cm) long and weigh more than 66 pounds (30 kg). They have sturdy little bodies with short legs and a long, flat, scaly tail. A beaver's tail may be as big as 18 inches (45 cm) long and 5 inches (12.7 cm) wide.

Beavers are graceful swimmers but move **awkwardly** on land. They make their homes in freshwater **environments** such as ponds, rivers, and streams. They're mostly nocturnal, meaning that they're active at night rather than during the daytime.

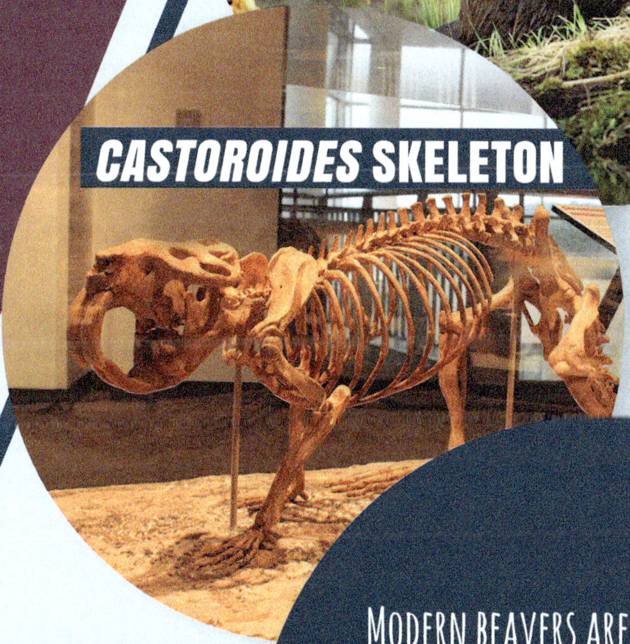

Modern beavers are relatives of a prehistoric animal called *Castoroides*, or the giant beaver. Giant beavers are believed to have been about 8 feet (2.4 m) long and may have weighed up to 220 pounds (100 kg). That's as big as a black bear!

BEAVERS AND TREES

Beavers are herbivores, meaning they only eat plants. One of a beaver's favorite foods is cambium, which is the inner bark of a tree. During the fall, beavers hide away branches and twigs to eat in the winter. They'll also eat roots, grass, and water plants.

Beavers chew down trees both to eat their bark and to cut them into pieces to use for building dams and lodges. Trees used for dam building usually measure about 4 to 12 inches (10.2 to 30.5 cm) across. However, the biggest recorded tree to be cut down by beavers was 110 feet (33.5 m) tall!

Some trees used by beavers include willow, poplar, and cottonwood trees.

TOOLS OF THE TRADE

A beaver's body is **equipped** with all the tools it needs for building and getting around. Its sharp teeth have a coating that contains iron, which makes them orange. Beavers use their strong teeth to chop down trees. They use their wide flat tails to balance when on land and to slap the water to communicate.

They have small front feet with five toes and sharp claws. Their hind feet are webbed to help them paddle through the water quickly. They have special **glands** that release an oily substance, which they spread over their fur to make it waterproof.

A BEAVER'S EYES ARE COVERED WITH A CLEAR **MEMBRANE** THAT WORKS LIKE GOGGLES SO THAT THEY CAN SEE UNDERWATER. ITS NOSE AND EARS CLOSE UP TO KEEP WATER OUT.

GETTING TO WORK

Beavers build dams with a plan. They choose a spot where the water is shallow and doesn't move too quickly. They then build a base of rocks and mud across the water's path. The mud locks the rocks into place, making a sturdy foundation for the dam.

Beavers make their dams with sticks and tree trunks packed together with mud and plants. Beavers cut down trees using only their teeth. Behind their teeth, they have special lips that block water from getting into their mouth when they swim while carrying sticks. They pat grass and mud into place to make the dam waterproof.

BEAVERS CAN SWIM AS FAST AS FIVE MILES (8 KM) PER HOUR.

A finished dam can be 10 feet (3 m) tall. The longest dam ever found is about 0.9 mile (1.5 km) long!

WHY BUILD DAMS?

Beavers build dams to create better living conditions for themselves and their families. A dam blocks the flow of water, creating a small pond or wetland. Beavers build lodges within these areas.

Beavers are hunted by predators such as coyotes, which are much better at moving on land than beavers are. Beavers build their homes behind dams so a barrier of water keeps predators away. Dams also give beavers a safe area to store and look for food.

Beavers attack other beavers that enter their territory. They mark their territory with mud piles mixed with oil from their bodies.

Beavers build smaller dams within their territory to create safe spaces in which to look for food and carry it home.

A BEAVER'S LODGE

Beavers live in colonies made up of a male and female pair and their young. Beavers stay with their **mates** for life. Once a year, the female gives birth to a litter of up to nine babies.

The colony lives within the lodge, which has underwater entrances. Inside the lodge there's an above-water living space with a soft bed of grass and wood chips. The roof of the lodge has a narrow opening like a chimney to let in fresh air. The packed layers of mud and sticks keep heat inside, warming the living area on cold days.

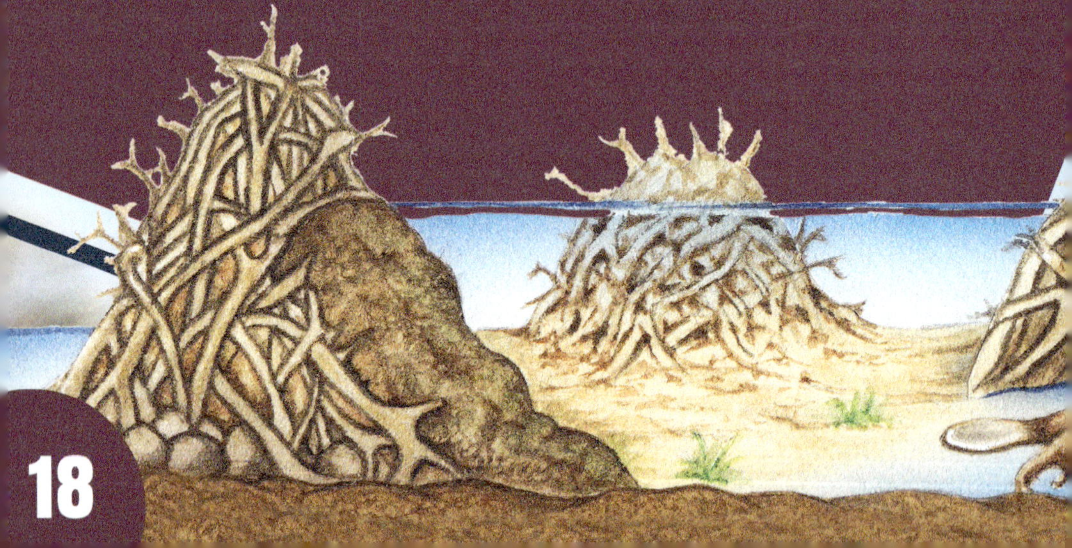

It takes a pair of beavers about a week to build a lodge, but they need to add to it and fix it regularly.

PROS AND CONS OF DAMS

Beaver dams are helpful in many ways. Ponds created by these dams provide homes for other animals and lead to healthy plant growth. Dams filter water and make it cleaner. They can prevent floods by slowing the flow of water. Dams also slow **erosion** and help healthy soil build up. They often lead to the creation of meadows.

Unfortunately, beavers and their dams can also cause problems and harm the environment. Beavers sometimes cut down too many trees. Dams can cause floods in places that cause problems for homeowners and farmers. People who live near beaver **habitats** might see them as a problem.

Some of the animals that live in dam pond **ecosystems** include salmon, trout, and frogs.

BENEFITS OF BEAVERS

Understanding more about beavers and their dams can help us create a better future for the environment. Efforts to save beavers have made sure they're no longer in danger of dying out. Beavers can be found in most parts of the United States and are protected by law from being overhunted.

Beaver dams are a part of rich, healthy ecosystems. Dams create ponds and wetlands that support many other plants and animals. They also filter water, create healthy soil, and control flooding. It's important that we don't **interfere** with the work of these busy little builders.

GLOSSARY

awkward: Clumsy or without grace.

ecosystem: A natural community of living and nonliving things.

engineering: The branch of technology concerned with designing and building.

environment: The natural world around us.

equipped: Prepared; having the supplies to do an activity.

erosion: The wearing away of Earth's surface by wind or water.

gland: A body part that produces something that helps with a bodily function.

habitat: The natural home for plants, animals, and other living things.

interfere: To disturb or prevent something.

mate: A partner for making babies, or to come together to make babies.

membrane: A soft, thin layer of living matter.

transform: To change something completely.

INDEX

WEBSITES

Due to the changing nature of Internet links, PowerKids Press has developed an online list of websites related to the subject of this book. This site is updated regularly. Please use this link to access the list:
www.powerkidslinks.com/ls/bea